YOU KNOW YOU'RE A CHILD OF THE '60s

WHEN...

MARK LEIGH
MIKE LEPINE

summersdale

YOU KNOW YOU'RE A CHILD OF THE '60s WHEN...

Copyright © Summersdale Publishers Ltd, 2006

All trademarks are acknowledged as belonging to their respective companies.

Text by Mark Leigh and Mike Lepine

Summersdale Publishers Ltd
46 West Street
Chichester
West Sussex
PO19 1RP
UK

www.summersdale.com

Printed and bound by Tien \

ISBN: 1-84024-515-8
ISBN: 978-1-84024-515-8

Mike Lepine

The 1960s was a time of free love, shameless promiscuity, openly expressed sexuality and carnal experimentation. Unfortunately, Mike Lepine was only nine when the '60s ended so he missed the bloody lot. Instead, his '60s were spent reading *Victor*, *Hotspur* and *Hornet* comics, devouring Witch's Hats from the Tonibell ice cream van and dressing up as Scott Tracy.

Mark Leigh

Born in 1966, Mark Leigh spent the Summer of Love wearing terry nappies and a bonnet rather than purple loon pants and a beaded headband. Like many children of his generation, he expected to grow up living under a dome on the moon, rather than in a four-bed semi in Surrey. Mark's biggest regrets, though, are that he never possessed a Crackerjack pencil or a Blue Peter badge.

THANK YOU TO

From Mike:
Philippa Hatton Lepine

From Mark:
Debbie, Polly, Barney and little sis Miri

You know you're a child of the '60s when...

You used to have flowers in your hair. Now it's Grecian 2000.

In any conversation about *The X Factor* you find yourself muttering about *Opportunity Knocks*.

You can still recall the names of all six firemen in *Trumpton* (OK, it's Pugh, Pugh, Barney McGrew, Cuthbert, Dibble and Grubb).

You were repeatedly told, 'Never trust The Man'. Too late, you found out that The Man in question is managing your pension fund.

You still think of Cuba as a base for soviet missiles and not a trendy package holiday destination.

In your heart you're still a free-spirited flower child – albeit a free-spirited flower child with a mortgage, 2.4 children and a nine-to-five job in IT.

You used to call everybody over 30 'Granddad'. It's not so funny now, is it?

You used to really want to marry that girl in the balloon from the Nimble advert. Her or Lady Penelope.

You once looked to India for spiritual enlightenment, rather than banking enquiries and train times.

Your first boyfriend said you looked just like Cilla Black – and you didn't take it as a gross insult.

You remember when there were only three TV channels – and they were only on for part of the day... yet there was *still* more good stuff to watch than on the Sky Multichannels package today.

Growing up as a girl, the only careers that were open to you involved typing, nursing or hairdressing.

If you were a boy, you really, really wanted to be an astronaut. Or a train driver.

You always used to know where north was as a child – as long as you took off one of your Clarks Commandos shoes and peeked at the hidden compass inside.

You can reminisce for hours about Magilla Gorilla, Ivor the Engine and Topo Gigio.

Your birthday cards usually contained a ten shilling note or a book token (and you were bloody grateful).

You once thought Cliff Richard was a rock 'n' roll rebel – until he entered the Eurovision Song Contest.

You're still sensitive about wearing glasses in case people start calling you Joe 90.

You remember
Nelson Mandela
going to prison.

Every visit to the Saturday morning pictures at the ABC would be spoiled by some crap made by the Children's Film Foundation (usually about go-carting and starring Dennis Waterman).

Your first pair of Levis cost one pound seventeen and six.

One of the TV shows you watched as a kid involved hapless hamsters and rats stuffed into miniature boats – and everyone found this very funny.

You sometimes
wonder how you ever
survived growing up
in a world without
airbags, seat belts
or childproof
medicine bottles.

You were never, ever convinced that the Milky Bar Kid was 'strong and tough'.

Your bible used to be *On the Road*. (Now it's a Haynes manual for your Vauxhall Vectra.)

You've enjoyed one summer of love – and over twenty summers of hosepipe bans.

You used to believe you'd be living on the moon by the twenty-first century. (The Brooke Bond Tea Cards lied...)

You had a mad granny who'd gleefully give you a ha'penny to go on holiday with and advise you – in all seriousness – not to spend it all at once.

THRUSH was the sworn enemy of the Man from U.N.C.L.E. – and not an inevitable fact of life.

All it took to
impress a girl
was a Babycham
followed by dinner
at a Berni Inn.

You're secretly proud of your Tufty Club membership.

It once took trips to at least eight different shops to get all the weekly groceries.

Your mum's kitchen radio was perpetually tuned to *Sing Something Simple* and *The Billy Cotton Band Show*.

You used to live in fear of the four-minute warning; now it's the feral kids off the local estate.

You have a vague memory of a BBC comedy that starred Terry Scott and Hugh Lloyd as two garden gnomes... or did you just imagine it?

The aerial of your dad's car had a woolly tiger tail attached to it.

You recall watching westerns where the cowboys would rope cattle and shoot guns, rather than have anal sex.

You blame sweet cigarettes and liquorice pipes for your current 60-a-day habit.

You remember when Carnaby Street attracted swinging cats, not gullible tourists.

Most of your toys came from Tri-ang, Matchbox or Chad Valley.

The most exotic dishes you'd ever tasted were prawn cocktail and black forest gateau.

You can still
remember when
British female tennis
players were good
(and plentiful).

The Pacemakers were a pop band who played with a bloke called Gerry – not essentials for your everyday living.

They used to tell you to 'go to work on an egg'. Bizarre advice – but these days an egg is still more likely to get you to work on time than South West Trains.

The biggest dilemma in your life used to be 'Zoom or Skyray?'

The Loneliness of the Long Distance Runner spoke to you.

You really believed
that Nice Girls Don't.

You used to watch *The Black and White Minstrel Show* and considered it good clean family fun, rather than a 'cultural obscenity'.

You can name at least ten of the people on the *Sergeant Pepper* album cover.

Your three favourite possessions were once a poster of Che Guevara, a Donovan album and a large orange bean bag.

You're solidly and
defiantly pre-metric
and still haven't
got a clue about
how long a kilo
is or how heavy a
centilitre might be.

You had your tonsils removed and woke up to ice cream rather than MRSA.

You still think John Lennon is the greatest person who ever lived – even after you found out about his penchant for urinating over nuns. Oh well, no one's perfect...

You watched *Harry Potter and The Chamber of Secrets* and admired the Ford Anglia 105E far more than the plot.

You actually took
the trouble to make
your own clothes.

The first erotic photo
you ever saw was
of Christine Keeler
sitting on a chair.

You were absolutely stunned that a contestant on *Double Your Money* could walk away with as much as £600.

You can remember lava lamps, parkas and the Mini... the first time round.

You recall the thrill of reading *Janet and John* – and being desperate to find out what happened when they went through the garden gate...

Your impression of the Germans and the Japanese is coloured by all those *War Picture Library* comics you used to read – as is your command of their languages. (Who knows – '*Banzai Aieeeee!*' may still come in handy.)

Your parents threatened to throw you out if you ever became a hippy.

Patience wasn't just a virtue: it was a necessity when TV sets took five minutes to warm-up.

You can still remember not only how to dance the Twist, but also the Hitch-Hike, the Watusi, the Chicken and the Mashed Potato.

You learned
the facts of life
from playground
rumours and your
older brother's
copy of *Health
and Efficiency*.

The opening sequences to *Mission Impossible* and *The Banana Splits* are indelibly stamped on your brain.

You remember George Best more for hitting the back of the net than hitting the bottle.

You'd happily occupy yourself for hours with a packet of pipe cleaners, paper clips and some cereal boxes trying to create some totally useless item like they made on *Blue Peter*.

Walking home from school was relatively safe; no one ever got mugged for their new plimsolls.

Your first crush was the boy at the funfair who took the money on the Waltzer.

You know the
difference between
Mr Spock and
Dr Spock.

The biggest playground status symbol was owning a 'Johnny Seven' (seven guns in one!).

You remember your granny getting strangely excited when Jackie Pallo turned up on the wrestling.

You got all your
funniest lines
from Ken Dodd.

Being caned or having a blackboard rubber thrown at your head were a perfectly acceptable part of school life, not a precursor to your teacher being suspended and splashed all over the *Mail on Sunday*.

D. I. Barlow was the dirtiest, meanest cop you'd ever seen on television.

Your John Collier
charge card
marked you out
as a high roller.

Playing conkers was more popular than playing truant.

You bought all your singles from Boots the Chemist.

The three most significant letters in your life used to be CND. Now it's RSI.

You were entertained
by the adventures
of a bush kangaroo
that was really just
Lassie with a pouch.

You still remember a thrilling sense of anticipation watching *Grandstand*'s teleprinter displaying the latest football results.

You remember a time before retro.

The answer was 'blowing in the wind' – not 42.

You used to have really long hair – just not growing out of your nose and ears.

Your Sundays were once spent at a 'happening' and not a car boot sale.

You can't walk over
Waterloo Bridge
without thinking of
Terry and Julie.

You still wonder what was so wrong with John Tracy that International Rescue deliberately kept him up in space alone on Thunderbird Five all the time. (Body odour? Unnatural interest in Grandma Tracy?)

You still know all the words to the theme song of *Casey Jones* ('... a steamin' and a rollin'...').

It's been over 35 years – and you still can't fathom what that last episode of *The Prisoner* was all about.

Mary Hopkins sang 'Those Were the Days' – and you didn't know then how right she was.

www.summersdale.com